QUICK LAUNCH FORMULA

THE

7-DAY

ENTREPRENEUR

Turn Your Side Hustle Or Million-Dollar Idea Into A Reality In 1 Week

MITCHE GRAF

Interested in more books by Mitche?

https://amzn.to/4f4ziAL

Interested in hiring Mitche to speak?

https://powermarketing101.com/speaking

Interested in joining Mitche's MasterMind?

https://powermarketing101.com/coaching

Dedication

This book is dedicated to my youngest kid, Sierra, who has always been my little sidekick for my adventures in life. Always smiling, constantly wanting to spend time with me, and completely interested in what Dad has going on in his life. She's not allowed to date until she's 37, so I'm thinking she will be my sidekick for quite a while more...

I LOVE YOU!

Dad

THE 7-DAY ENTREPRENEUR

Copyright © 2024 Mitche Graf.

All rights reserved.

Cover Design:

Back Cover Photo: Sierra Graf

Editor: Fatima Jemil

Publisher: Power Marketing 101

P.O. Box 405

Aurora, Oregon 97002 USA

FOR BULK ORDERS OR GROUP DISCOUNTS

CALL: 888.719.4692

www.MitcheGraf.com

ISBN: 979-8-9855833-6-6

About Your Captain For This Flight

Mitche Graf has been a lifestyle entrepreneur for over 35 years and has launched more businesses than some people have hot dinners. He has shown he's got the Midas touch for turning ideas into gold.

From hawking lemonade in the 3rd grade to running 4 companies today, He plans add to his tally of 12 businesses he's scaled and sold.

He also took a year off from running his own companies to become the President of a professional sports team, a Class A affiliate of the world-champion San Francisco Giants baseball team. In 2019, he led an organizational re-brand that had fans pouring in, boosting attendance by 12%, one of the largest increased in all of professional baseball.

Mitche has launched multiple award-winning restaurants, a bustling catering and events company, a national spice manufacturing business, an award-winning photography studio, and even a night crawler company. Because, why not? He's also founded a national cribbage board company, an award-winning limousine business, a portable hot tub rental service, a drive-through espresso company, an educational products company, a publishing agency, and an athletic fitness testing corporation.

As a radio host, Mitche's voice can be heard on *"The Business Edge Minute"* and *"The BBQ Radio Show,"* which air on over 150 radio stations nationwide combined. His quick wit and fast-paced style have made his shows hit the top 1% of all podcasts as well, earning them significant national press.

He's penned 12 books, covering everything from marketing espresso, to starting a business, to unleashing your inner ninja. His titles include:

- "Marketing Your Espresso Business" (1994)
- "Power Marketing, Selling & Pricing" (2004) - Best Seller
- "The Passionate Life: A Common Man's Dream To Getting Anything You Want Out Of Everything You Do" (2009)
- "The Unleashed Entrepreneur: A KickAss Guide To Harnessing Your Inner Ninja, Working Less, & Building The Lifestyle Of Your Dreams" (2018) - Best Seller

- "BBQ Unleashed Recipe Book" (2018)
- "High Voltage Branding: Go from Ordinary to Extra-Ordinary" (2020)
- "The Business Basics BootCamp: The Ultimate Crash Course" (2020) – International Best Seller
- "Entertain Like a Pro: Appetizers" (2020)
- "Customer Service Is DEAD: Delivering 6-Star Service in A 1-Star World" (2021) International Best Seller
- "Snuggles, Kisses & Hugs Have a Party" (written with his 7-year-old daughter Sierra) (2021)
- "Put Down Your Freakin' Phone: Reboot Your Thinking, Transform Your Life, & Conquer The Sky Dragons In Your Backyard" (2024)

He has taught his high-voltage seminars and workshops to over 105,000 people in nine countries and nearly every U.S. state (sorry, Maine!). He's earned his PhD from The School of Hard Knocks, with a major in "Getting Punched in the Face by Failure." His failures have been his best teachers, but he has always come back swinging. From his business highs to bankruptcy in the early 90's, Mitche has always fought tooth and nail to carve out a niche for himself, regardless of what industry he was dabbling in at the time.

When he's not revolutionizing the business world, Mitche is all about work-life balance. He loves the outdoors, playing guitar, cooking, enjoying good wine, and spending lots of time with his kids. He volunteers as the PA Announcer for 4 varsity sports at the local high school, and in his free time, you might find him fishing, gold panning, gardening, telling bad Dad jokes, or writing songs with his guitar.

Living in a small town in Oregon, Mitche is the proud daddy of three incredible kids, Jaycee, Colton, and Sierra. His household also includes dogs Tilly and Delilah, a lizard named Opa, and several hundred guppies (names not important). His motto is "work less, live more," so he can focus on what truly matters. For Mitche, every day is a Saturday.

For speaking inquiries, please contact All American Speakers Bureau by calling 888-719-4692 or visiting- https://www.allamericanspeakers.com/

Mitche can lecture on a vast plethora of topics including delivering 6-star customer service, entrepreneurship, starting a business, branding, marketing, time management, lifestyle design, work/life balance, motivation, selling a business, and controlling social media.

Table of Contents

Introduction

My first entrepreneurial bug infested me when I was in grade school.

I remember selling lemonade on Saturday mornings on the sidewalk in front of my house, with a table and chairs, and an AM transistor radio playing Los Angeles Dodger games. Yes, I said Dodgers games.

The other kids in the neighborhood would sell their lemonade for .25, but I sold mine for .50, gave you a free cookie, AND the added bonus of Dodger games being blasted on a little round green transistor radio in the background. In fact, I still have the old radio on a shelf in my office as a reminder of those times...and I'm still a BIG Dodger fan.

I always seemed to have more people lined up to buy my lemonade even though I charged double what everyone else was charging. Even at that young age, I had figured out a basic truth about the entrepreneurial journey: if you want to be successful, you must find ways to add value to your product or service that exceeds expectations. If you can do this, magic things will start to happen, and you will be on the road to massive success!

That's when I had my first spark.

If you ask any entrepreneur when their first spark appeared, they will be able to recall the exact moment and the exact day it happened.

If you are reading this book, that tells me that you also have a spark deep inside of your soul- or perhaps you are looking for one.

Having a desire to be your own boss is indeed a special calling, and it definitely isn't for everyone. If you are hearing that calling, you are one of the chosen few who have been selected to make a real difference in the world around you. This is a BIG deal and cause for celebration!

THE 7-DAY ENTREPRENEUR

We're living in a golden age for entrepreneurs. The barriers to entry have never been lower, and the tools you need to start a business are literally at your fingertips. Whether you're starting a side hustle, launching a full-fledged business, or just exploring how to make money doing what you love, this is the perfect time to dive in. Why? Because the world is changing—and it's changing fast.

Technology has leveled the playing field. Gone are the days when you needed a ton of capital or fancy office space to get started. You can build a website from your couch or at the beach, reach millions through social media, and offer services worldwide from the comforts of your smartphone. Add in the rise of the gig economy, remote work culture, and people's increasing desire to support small businesses, and you've got a recipe for success just waiting for you to take the first step.

The world is shifting, and opportunity is everywhere. The COVID-19 pandemic showed us that traditional jobs aren't as secure as we once thought. People were forced to pivot, and many turned to their side hustles or hobbies to make ends meet. A lot of those people never looked back. They found out they could make money, a lot more money, by turning their passions into a business.

The digital economy is booming, e-commerce is exploding, and people are craving new, authentic, and personalized experiences. That's where YOU come in. You have something unique to offer, whether it's a skill, a product, or an idea that the world needs. And right now, the world is primed to say, "Yes, I want what you're offering."

Maybe you're passionate about cooking, photography, playing cribbage, gardening, or you've always been the go-to person for fixing tech issues. Maybe you're a great baker, fitness guru, or artist. Whatever your thing is, people are looking for solutions, and they're willing to pay for what you do best. The question is: are you ready to meet that demand?

That's where this book comes in. Over the next seven days, we're going to break down the essential steps to turn your side hustle or million-dollar idea into something tangible and real. Think of this as your 7-day entrepreneurial bootcamp—each day packed with practical, easy-to-follow advice that will get you closer to your goal.

And don't worry, I won't bog you down with complicated jargon or endless theories. This book is all about action.

Take a copious number of notes, lots of notes, an insane amount of notes! If you write something down, you are much more likely to act on it verses simply reading it on the page.

I want you to vomit all of your thoughts onto the page, brainstorm and "spit wad" with family members or friends, and squeeze out every last drop of juice out of your idea as you go through the mental exercises in this book.

I've been an entrepreneur for over 35 years, but I've never bought into the outdated "work 24/7 to be successful" mindset. I believe in working smart, not hard. I run multiple businesses, but here's the kicker—I have a different definition of what 24/7 means. To me it means working 24 hours a week, 7 months a year, and that's how I set up my life. set up my lifestyle to work 24 hours a week, 7 months a year.

Am I successful with this? Not all of the time, but that's my shining beacon on the hill. It forces me to be uber-efficient with my time and focus on the activities that actually move the needle on my businesses. I challenge you to approach this book with the same mindset...putting your lifestyle first, and then figuring out what your business blueprint needs to look like. It's reverse-engineering the process.

What do I do with the rest of the time? I enjoy life. I hang out with my family, coach my kids' sports teams, play guitar, a, garden, fish, and live my life by design, not by default.

I learned early on that if you hire smart people around you, pay them well and stay out of their way, you can build something sustainable without sacrificing your sanity. So, I'm living proof that you don't need to grind yourself into the ground to be a successful entrepreneur. It's all about efficiency and focus—knowing what to prioritize and how to delegate the rest.

As you go through this book, I want you to keep this philosophy in the front of your mind.

No matter where you are in your journey—whether you're just starting to toy with the idea of a side hustle or you've been sitting on your business idea for years—it's time to take action. The world isn't going to wait for you to get ready. You've got to jump in and learn as you go.

It's time to flame your spark and turn it into a roaring flame.

So, my suggestion is that you turn off your phone, grab some snacks, and find somewhere to hole up for a couple of hours and immerse yourself in this book.

Buckle up, buttercup! It's going to be a wild ride!

Chapter 1

The Entrepreneurial Mindset (Day 1)

What You Need to Succeed

To begin, what is your definition of an entrepreneur? If you've got visions of a slick business mogul in a fancy suit, sitting in a skyscraper corner office and sipping overpriced coffee while signing million-dollar deals—let's go ahead and shatter that myth right now.

Being an entrepreneur isn't about looking the part or fitting some specific mold. You don't need to be born into wealth, have an MBA, or wear a three-piece suit to be successful. I've started more than one business wearing nothing but sweatpants and a coffee-stained t-shirt. Lots of coffee stains.

In fact, the beauty of entrepreneurship is that it's open to anyone. Whether you're a stay-at-home parent with a great idea, a college student with a side hustle, or someone who's been working the same job for 20 years but feels that itch to do something more—there's a path for you. It's not about what you have right now or even what you know. It's about your mindset.

Being an entrepreneur is all about solving problems. You see something that could be done better, faster, or more creatively, and you figure out a way to make it happen. Entrepreneurs are people who don't wait for permission to start—they just do it. They take risks, make mistakes, and learn on the fly. Anyone can be an entrepreneur if they're willing to adopt this mindset.

Demystifying the Myth

Let's bust a common myth while we're at it: there's no "entrepreneurial gene." It's not like you have to be born with a special talent for business, like those kids who were selling lemonade at five years old and owning a car dealership by 15. When I started out, I wasn't exactly Steve Jobs. In fact, one of my first entrepreneurial ventures was a classic case of "learning the hard way."

I was fresh out of the 6th grade and I thought I'd hit the jackpot by selling used bicycle parts from my garage. I had this grand vision of turning my neighborhood into a cycling hub, where people would flock to buy their next set of banana seats, wheels or repair their old ones. I imagined fame, fortune, and maybe even a feature in the local paper. None of that happened. My "big idea" resulted in a garage full of dusty parts, and a little less cash than I started with.

That experience taught me something important: entrepreneurship isn't about instant success. It's about persistence. It's about seeing opportunities where others see problems. And most importantly, it's about bouncing back from failure with even more determination than before.

Anyone Can Be an Entrepreneur
Being an entrepreneur doesn't mean you have to create the next Facebook or invent a new piece of tech that changes the world. It can be as simple as turning your love for baking into a side business selling cookies or using your knack for fixing things to start a handyman service. Entrepreneurs come in all shapes, sizes, and

backgrounds. The only thing they all have in common is a willingness to take the plunge, try something new, and keep going even when things don't go exactly as planned.

It's not about being the smartest person in the room. It's about being the person who's willing to ask, "Why not?" and then figuring out the answer as they go. So, if you've been sitting there thinking that entrepreneurship is only for a select few or that you don't have what it takes, think again. You've got everything you need, right inside that head of yours.

If I can do it, believe me when I say that ANYONE can do it!

What You Really Need to Succeed

To succeed as an entrepreneur, you don't need a big bank account, endless free time, or even a business degree. Every successful entrepreneur you've ever heard of started out exactly where you are now, with a blank canvas, some passion, and a willingness to try.

As we dive into this 7-day journey, remember this: you already have what it takes. You just need to unlock it.

The Entrepreneurial Attitude

If you're going to jump into this wild world of building something from scratch, you need to pack a few essentials: resilience, adaptability, and maybe that proverbial good cup of coffee (or three).

The truth is, starting a new venture is kind of like playing a game of whack-a-mole. You'll knock one challenge down, only to have another 2 more pop up somewhere else. It's easy to get discouraged when things don't go according to plan—which, let's be honest, is most of the time. But that's where resilience comes in. It's the ability to bounce back, to keep going even when it feels like the world (or your new business) is conspiring against you.

I've had my fair share of setbacks. One of my first businesses was a portable hot tub rental company when I was in my late twenties. Yes, you heard that right...a portable hot tub rental business. I called it "Hot Tubs To Go" and the idea was that people could rent a hot tub on wheels for a weekend, and we'd set it up in their driveway.

The hot tub was placed on a flatbed, complete with railings, a carpeted deck, and of course the best sound system this side of on AC/DC concert. How could it fail, right?

What I didn't anticipate was just how many logistics go into moving hot tubs, the amount of chemicals and propane to heat the water, let alone keeping them clean, maintaining the equipment, and getting customers to actually *rent* them. That actually was the easiest part of the business, getting people to fork up $225 for a 3-day rental (Friday afternoon until Monday morning). With my background in selling, we had booking out several months in advance, but that's where the easy stuff ended. It wasn't exactly the relaxing, soak-in-success business I envisioned.

I imagined selling franchises to every city in America. Dream big, right? I spent lots of money on franchise attorney fees, paid an architect for cool designs for my "good, better, best" models, not to mention the amount of time I invested in the process.

Did I make money? Absolutely! But I should have just kept my vision on a smaller level, and not had the grandiose dreams of dominating the globe. Bottom line, the idea didn't work all that well.

Even today, I think this business has great potential! If you are reading this now, maybe you are the one to carry the torch in the future? You never know...

Did I throw in the towel after the first challenge? No. I pivoted (a fancy word for "I tried something else"), learned what didn't work, and eventually moved on to other ventures. Resilience isn't about never failing, it's about being willing to get back up and try again, learning from the mistakes that were made, and then being ok with making NEW mistakes! It's all part of the entrepreneurial game.

Adaptability is equally important. You have to be willing to adjust when things aren't going your way. In the world of entrepreneurship, flexibility is your best friend. Your business plan might be a blueprint, but you've got to be ready to scribble in the margins and adjust as you go. Markets change, customer needs shift, and sometimes, you'll just have to roll with the punches.

And here's where it gets fun, being adaptable also means you get to be creative in your problem-solving. When something doesn't work out, it's an opportunity to think outside the box and come up with a solution you might not have considered before.

So, when you hit your first obstacle (and trust me, you will), don't freak out. Take a breath, laugh it off if you can, and get ready to pivot like a seasoned entrepreneur. Resilience and adaptability aren't just nice-to-haves, they're essential tools in your entrepreneurial toolkit.

Defining Your Why

Before you dive headfirst into the exciting world of entrepreneurship, you need to answer one big question: **Why are you doing this?** Your "why" is the driving force behind your journey. It's the fuel that keeps you going when things get tough, and there will be days when you feel like you're driving a car with three wheels and no GPS. On those days, your "why" is what gets you back on track.

It's your reason for starting this whole adventure. Maybe you're sick of your 9-to-5 and crave the freedom of working on your own terms. Maybe you want to spend more time with your family, or you're driven by the desire to solve a problem in the world. Whatever it is, your "why" is personal to you, and it's what will give you the motivation to keep going when challenges start piling up like emails on a Monday morning.

Let me tell you about my "why." When I first started out, I wasn't just chasing success—I was chasing a *lifestyle*. I didn't want to work myself to the bone for 80 hours a week and miss out on the important parts of life. I had a job as the National Sales Manager for a large pet products manufacturing company with about 40 inside salespeople and 12 outside reps. Great money, lots of benefits, but I had slowly given into the "just 1 more hour" philosophy and before I knew it I had a 7-day a week job. Not fun.

I then decided that I wanted to be the one that controlled my time, my income, and my future. That was back in the early 1990's and I haven't looked back since.

Then I met the woman of my dreams, had 3 wonderful kids, and my focus even became more clear than ever before.

I never want to miss a soccer game, a football game or track meet, or something as simple as a family BBQ on Saturday. I want to design my life in a way that allows me to work smart, not hard. My "why" was (and still is) about freedom, freedom to enjoy life, freedom to build businesses on my own terms, and freedom to *not* answer emails at 11 p.m. on a Friday. That's what keeps me going.

When your "why" is strong enough, it becomes your superpower. It helps you push through the hard times, those moments when you're questioning if you've completely lost your mind for starting a business. Your "why" is what you'll lean on when fear, doubt, and uncertainty creep in. It's your North Star, guiding you through the storms.

The "Why" Exercise

Grab that notebook (yes, I'm serious—grab it!) and let's define your "why." This is the reason you're embarking on this journey. Write down your answer to these questions:

> **Why do I want to start this side hustle?** Is it about financial freedom, time freedom, pursuing a passion, or maybe proving something to yourself?

> **What do I hope to achieve?** Think about what success looks like for you—whether that's quitting your day job, paying off debt, or making an impact in your community.

> **What am I willing to endure to get there?** Entrepreneurship isn't all sunshine and rainbows. Be honest about what challenges you're ready to tackle.

> **What fears or doubts do I have?** Write them down, and then next to each fear, jot down how you plan to overcome it. If you're worried about failing, ask yourself, "What's the worst that can happen, and how can I bounce back?"

By the time you've answered these questions, you'll have a clear sense of what's driving you. And trust me, knowing your "why" will give you the energy to push through the inevitable obstacles.

Now that you've defined your "why," the next step is figuring out what lights your fire. In the next Chapter, we're going to dig deep into your passions and find the niche where your skills, interests, and market opportunities intersect. Your "why" will fuel your journey, but your passion and niche will be the engine that drives your side hustle forward.

Chapter 2:

Finding Your Passion & Niche (Day 2)

Turning Passion into Profit

Now it's time to figure out what sets your soul on fire and, more importantly, how to make some money from it. This is where the magic happens, taking something you love, something that excites you, and turning it into a business that puts cash in your pocket.

No matter how much you love knitting scarves or building model airplanes, doing it for free doesn't quite have the same ring as making money from it.

Passion is that thing you can't stop thinking about, even when you should probably be doing something else, like sleeping or cleaning the garage. It's the activity that makes hours fly by like minutes. Maybe it's BBQing, pottery, woodworking, fitness, or fixing things around the house. Whatever it is, if it lights you up and you'd do it even if no one paid you, that's a passion.

Just because you love something doesn't automatically mean people will pay for it. But don't let that kill your vibe just yet. The key is to find where your passion overlaps with a market need. That sweet spot is where side hustles turn into profitable businesses. Take something you love and figure out how it can solve a problem, make someone's life easier, or provide value in some way. Because people are willing to pay for solutions, and your passion might just be the perfect answer.

Side Hustles That Started Small

Let's look at some real-life examples of successful businesses that started as side hustles, just to get your creative wheels turning. Remember Spanx? Yeah, those wildly popular undergarments that make millions of women feel like superheroes? They started in Sara Blakely's living room with $5,000 and an idea. She didn't have a fashion degree or any experience in design. What she *did* have was a problem—her white pants didn't look flattering, and traditional shapewear wasn't cutting it. So, she turned her frustration into a solution, and Spanx was born.

Or how about Etsy, the online marketplace for handmade goods? It started as a way for artists and crafters to sell their creations on the side. Fast forward, and it's now a multi-billion dollar platform that helps thousands of people turn their hobbies into thriving businesses. The founders didn't have grand ambitions of taking over the world—they just saw an opportunity to bring creators and buyers together. And that's the key: they took their passion for unique, handmade items and found a way to deliver that to a market ready to pay for it.

And here's my personal favorite: a guy I know started out mowing lawns for his neighbors as a teenager. He didn't have fancy equipment or a big budget, just a love for being outdoors and making things look nice. Fast forward a few years, and his small lawn care side hustle turned into a full-fledged landscaping business with multiple crews, a shop full of vehicles and equipment, loads of clients, and lots of time off in the winters to ski in Europe with his family. Not too shabby for a passion that started with a lawnmower.

Think Outside the Box

If you're sitting there thinking, "Well, I'm not going to invent the next Spanx or become a lawn care mogul," don't worry. This isn't about replicating someone else's success; it's about finding your own path. Your passion doesn't need to be grand or revolutionary; it just needs to be something you love that can solve a problem for others.

And don't be afraid to get a little creative. I once met a guy who turned his passion for collecting vintage typewriters into a profitable side business. He refurbished and sold them to collectors and hipster coffee shops (because of course hipster coffee shops love vintage typewriters). Was it something most people would think of? Probably not. Did it work? You bet.

The point is, your passion might be a little quirky or niche, but that's what makes it special. Embrace it. In fact, the more specific and unique your passion, the better chance you have of standing out in a crowded market.

Exercise: Brainstorm Your Passions

Here's where you get to have a little fun. Grab your notebook, and make a list of everything you're passionate about—no matter how silly or obscure it might seem. Don't hold back. Write down your hobbies, skills, things you'd do for free, and the stuff you just can't stop thinking about.

Once you've got your list, circle the top three passions that get you the most excited. Now, for each of those, ask yourself:

> ➢ **How can I turn this into something people will pay for?**
> ➢ **What problem does this solve for others?**
> ➢ **Is there a market for this passion, or can I create one?**

By the end of this exercise, you'll have a better idea of which passions have the potential to be more than just a hobby—and that's where the magic starts to happen.

Narrowing Your Focus

When you're just starting out, it's tempting to try and be everything to everyone. You've got all these great ideas, and you're thinking, "Why not just offer *all* of them?" Well, trying to do everything at once is like going to a buffet with a giant plate and piling on lasagna, sushi, and a burger all at the same time. You might be excited to try it all, but it quickly turns into a messy, confusing disaster. The same thing happens with businesses that don't focus, they get overwhelmed, and the result is far from what you expected.

That's why niching down, focusing on a specific audience and a specific problem, is so important. The more narrowly you define your niche, the easier it is to stand out and connect with your ideal customers. When you try to appeal to everyone, you end up appealing to no one. But when you focus on a specific group of people, with a specific problem that *you* can solve, magic happens. You become the go-to expert for that niche, and suddenly, your business has direction and momentum.

Why Niche Down?

Think about it this way: if you're passionate about fitness, you could start a general fitness business. But so could a million other people. If you niche down and focus on something more specific, like helping busy moms regain their fitness postpartum, you've just narrowed your audience, and that's a good thing. You're no longer competing with everyone else in the general fitness world. Instead, you're speaking directly to a group of people who are looking for exactly what you offer.

Don't be afraid to start small and get hyper-specific with your audience. There's plenty of room for growth once you've nailed your niche. Besides, trying to be everything to everyone will just lead to burnout, confusion, and possibly a few sleepless nights where you wonder why you didn't listen to that book that told you to niche down. That would be this book, in case you were wondering.

Exercise: Narrow Your Niche

Grab your notebook again (I told you this book would keep you busy!) and take another look at those passions and ideas you brainstormed earlier. Now, for each one, ask yourself these questions:

- ➤ **Who needs this the most?**
- ➤ **What specific group of people could benefit from this?**
- ➤ **How can I tailor my offering to serve a smaller, more focused audience?**

By the end of this exercise, you'll have a clearer idea of your niche. It might feel counterintuitive to narrow your focus, but trust me, this is the key to standing out and building a business that people can't wait to work with.

And remember, starting small doesn't mean thinking small. It just means you're setting yourself up for bigger wins down the road.

Validating Your Idea

You've got your passion, you've narrowed down your niche, and you're feeling pretty excited. But before you start designing business cards and ordering branded coffee mugs, you need to validate your idea. In other words, you need to test whether your idea actually has legs before you dive headfirst into it. Think of it like dipping your toe in the water before committing to a full cannonball.

Simple Ways to Test Your Idea

Validating your business idea doesn't have to be complicated or expensive. In fact, it's easier than you might think. The goal is to gather real-world feedback to see if people are actually interested in what you're offering, and if they're willing to pay for it.

Here are a few simple ways to get started:

1. **Ask Your Target Audience**: If you've already narrowed down your niche, start by talking to the people who fit that description. This can be as simple as reaching out to friends, family, or acquaintances who fall into your target market. Ask them if they'd be interested in your product or service. Better yet, ask if they'd be willing to *pay* for it. Their reactions will give you a good idea of whether your idea has potential.

2. **Run a Survey**: You don't need to be a data scientist to run a quick survey. Tools like Google

Forms or SurveyMonkey let you create free surveys in minutes. Send the survey to your social media followers, email contacts, or any relevant online groups. Ask questions like: *Would you use this product or service? What problem would this solve for you? How much would you pay for it?*

3. **Create a Simple Landing Page**: Before you fully commit, set up a basic landing page that describes your product or service. Include a call-to-action, like "Sign up for more information" or "Pre-order now." If people are interested enough to give you their email or make a commitment, you know you're onto something.

Gathering Feedback

When it comes to gathering feedback, the key is to listen with an open mind. Sometimes, the feedback might not be exactly what you want to hear, but that's okay, it's better to learn now than after you've poured a bunch of time and money into something no one really wants. Keep asking questions and be open to tweaking your idea based on what you hear.

I'll give you a quick example from my own experience. Back in the day, I had this brilliant (or so I thought) idea to start a gourmet meal delivery service. I was convinced people would pay top dollar to have restaurant-quality meals delivered to their door. This was way before DoorDash and GrubHub.

So, I put together some sample menus and asked a few people in my target market what they thought. The feedback? "Uh, sounds great, but I'm not paying that much for something I could just pick up from a restaurant."

But instead of throwing in the towel, I adjusted. I simplified the meals, cut down on the fancy ingredients, and came up with a more affordable plan. That feedback ended up shaping the entire business model and making it a success. If I hadn't taken the time to validate my idea, I might've ended up with a lot of gourmet meals and no one to eat them. Over the next few years, this idea eventually blossomed into a 100-seat restaurant and a very busy catering business with over 60 employees.

By validating your idea, you're giving yourself a solid foundation to build on.

THE 7-DAY ENTREPRENEUR

Chapter 3

The MVP: Minimum Viable Product (Day 3)

The Power of an MVP

You've validated your idea and you're ready to bring it to life. But before you go all-in, let me introduce you to one of the most important concepts in entrepreneurship: the **Minimum Viable Product**, or MVP. This is going to save you a lot of time, money, and headaches.

An MVP is the smallest, most basic version of your product or service that you can create and test with real customers. It's not about launching a perfectly polished product on day one; it's about getting a working version out there quickly to see how the market responds. The idea behind an MVP is to start small, gather feedback, and then improve as you go. This way, you're not wasting resources building something no one wants or needs.

Why Start Small?

An MVP allows you to test the waters without diving headfirst into the deep end. The beauty of an MVP is that it keeps you flexible and pliable. Instead of spending months (or years) perfecting something in isolation, you get immediate feedback from real customers. If they love it, great! You can build on that momentum. If they don't, it's a lot easier to make adjustments when you're only working with the bare essentials.

You're also not stuck with a massive product or service that no one wants, and you avoid the common entrepreneurial trap of "perfecting" something before it even sees the light of day.

An MVP in Action

Of all the mistakes I've seen new entrepreneurs make, the biggest one is waiting until their product is perfect in every way, or 100% developed.

Let's take a look at an example of a business that started with an MVP and turned it into something huge. When Dropbox's founders first came up with the idea for their cloud storage service, they didn't build a full-blown product right away. Instead, they created a simple explainer video that demonstrated how Dropbox would work. That's it, a video. There wasn't even a working product behind it yet.

The video, which was shared online, generated massive interest. People started signing up for the service before it even existed. With this early feedback, the founders knew they were onto something. Only then did they go ahead and build the actual product. Today, Dropbox is worth billions, and it all started with nothing more than a basic MVP, a video that tested the waters before diving into full development.

The key takeaway here? Starting small doesn't mean thinking small. By focusing on an MVP, you're giving yourself room to grow, adapt, and respond to your customers' needs. And in the world of entrepreneurship, that kind of flexibility is gold.

Creating Your MVP

Now that you understand the power of an MVP, it's time to roll up your sleeves and create your own. Remember, you don't need to be a perfectionist. In fact, the whole point is to *not* aim for perfection. Your MVP isn't about bells and whistles, it's about creating the simplest, bare-bones version of your product or service that solves the core problem for your customers.

The mantra you want to keep in mind? **Start small, think big.**

What Does an MVP Look Like?

Your MVP is the basic version of what you're offering. Let's say your passion is baking, and you want to start a custom cake business. Your MVP isn't a fully operational bakery with 20 flavors and a full website with online ordering. It's just you, a licensed kitchen, a few cakes, and maybe a simple Instagram page. The goal is to make a few cakes, see how people respond, and gather feedback. Maybe start with just three cake options—basic but delicious—and offer them to friends, family, or local events. That's your MVP.

If you're thinking of offering a service, the same concept applies. Maybe you want to start a graphic design business. Your MVP could be a simple one-page website or even just a social media profile where you showcase a few samples of your work. You don't need a portfolio of 50 designs or a fancy, expensive website right now. Just create a few designs, share them, and see what potential clients say.

Keep It Simple

The trick to creating your MVP is to avoid getting bogged down in details or trying to make everything perfect right away. **Your MVP isn't the final version of your product or service**, it's the first draft. And like all first drafts, it's going to have a few rough edges. That's totally okay. You're not aiming for a flawless product; you're aiming for a working version that does its job, even if it's a little rough around the edges.

Think of it like building a house. You're not worrying about the fancy crown molding or the imported Italian tile floors just yet—you're putting up the walls and making sure the roof doesn't leak. You can always add the finishing touches later. For now, focus on getting something out there that your target audience can use, experience, and give you feedback on.

Action Step: Build Your MVP

Grab that trusty notebook again and write down the simplest version of your product or service that you can launch right now. Ask yourself:

- **What's the core problem my product or service solves?**
- **What's the absolute minimum I need to create in order to solve that problem?**

By the end of this exercise, you'll have a clear idea of what your MVP looks like. Remember, this is just the beginning. You can always add, improve, and polish later. For now, get it out there and let the real-world feedback guide you.

And don't stress if it's not perfect, if Dropbox could launch with just a video, you're more than ready to test your idea with something simple. Now that you've built your MVP, the next step is getting it out into the world and improving as you go. But for now, just focus on taking that first step. It doesn't have to be perfect—it just has to be *done*.

Feedback is Gold

Congratulations! You've built your MVP and you're ready to release it into the wild. But before you throw a party to celebrate, there's one crucial step that will shape the success of your venture: **getting feedback**. And not just any feedback, real, honest feedback from the people who are going to use your product or service. Because here's the thing: what you think is amazing might need a few tweaks (or let's be real, sometimes a complete overhaul) before it's ready for prime time. But don't worry, that's a good thing.

Why Feedback is Your Best Friend

In the world of entrepreneurship, **feedback is absolute gold**. It's your secret weapon for creating a product or service that people will love. Think of it as your personal GPS: without it, you might be driving in the wrong direction, wasting time, energy, and possibly cash. But with the right feedback, you can adjust your course early and often, making sure you're on track to success.

Remember, your MVP is like the first draft of a book. It's good, but it's not perfect yet. And that's okay! That's why feedback exists—to help you improve and refine before you fully commit. Early testers can tell you what's working, what's confusing, and what could be better. With their input, you'll be able to make adjustments and avoid the painful (and expensive) mistake of launching something that doesn't resonate.

When gathering feedback, ask questions that will give you actionable insights. Here are a few to get you started:

- o What do you like about this product/service?
- o What's confusing or unclear?
- o What would make this better?
- o Would you pay for this? If not, why?

By the end of this exercise, you'll have valuable feedback to work with, and you'll be able to fine-tune your MVP into something even more powerful. And remember, **it's okay if it's not perfect right away**, that's the whole point of the MVP process. You're learning and improving as you go.

Keep your MVP simple and let the feedback guide you, because next up, we're diving into how to turn that basic MVP into a **memorable brand** that stands out, without breaking the bank.

THE 7-DAY ENTREPRENEUR

Chapter 4

Building a Brand on a Budget (Day 4)

High Voltage Branding

When you hear the word "branding," what comes to mind? A catchy logo? A memorable tagline? Maybe even that swoosh from a certain athletic company. **Branding is so much more than just a name or a logo**. It's the entire experience someone has when they interact with your business. It's how people feel when they think about your product or service. In other words, branding is the personality of your business.

Think about it like this: when you meet someone for the first time, their appearance might catch your attention, but it's their personality, their vibe that keeps you interested. Your brand works the same way. The name and logo might get people in the door, but your brand's values, tone, and how you make people feel are what keep them coming back.

What Makes a Good Brand?

Having a great logo helps (no pressure!), but your brand goes beyond what's on the surface. It's about creating a consistent and recognizable experience for your customers. Everything from the tone of your social media posts to the way you answer customer emails contributes to your brand. Your brand is the promise you're making to your customers, whether that's to provide them with the best homemade cookies in town or to deliver top-notch tech support without the jargon. A good brand does a few things for you:

1. **It's Consistent**: Whether it's the colors you use, your tone of voice, or your messaging, consistency builds trust. When customers know what to expect from you, they feel comfortable coming back.

2. **It's Authentic**: The best brands are genuine. Don't try to be something you're not. Your customers will appreciate you for your

uniqueness, whether you're quirky, professional, quick-witted, or fun-loving.

3. **It's Customer-Centric**: A strong brand focuses on solving a customer's problem or meeting their needs. People aren't just buying a product or service; they're buying a solution to something they care about.

Let's take a well-known brand to illustrate this: **Apple**. Yes, they've got that sleek logo, but Apple's brand isn't just about that iconic fruit with a bite taken out of it. Their brand is all about simplicity, innovation, and elegance.

When you buy an Apple product, you're not just buying a phone or a laptop, you're buying into the idea that this product is going to make your life simpler, more efficient, and, let's be honest, a little cooler. Apple's branding isn't just in the product itself; it's in their minimalist packaging, their user-friendly design, and even their customer service.

Have you ever been into one of Apple's "Genius Bars" and experienced something different than what you would have expected? That's the point.

Every touchpoint reinforces the same message: "We make technology that works seamlessly and beautifully."

I'm not saying you need to create the next Apple (unless that's your goal, in which case, go for it!), but the point is, **branding is about the entire customer experience**. It's about how people perceive you and the value you bring to their lives.

Your Turn: Define Your Brand in One Sentence

Now it's time to take what you've learned and start building your own brand. Grab that notebook again and write down what your brand is all about.

Here's the challenge: **define your brand in one sentence**. Yes, just one sentence! It might sound tricky, but this exercise will help you focus on the core of what makes your business special.

Here are a few questions to help you get started:

- What problem(s) are you solving for your customers?
- What makes you unique in your market?

- How do you want people to feel when they interact with your business?

By the time you finish, you should have a clear, concise statement that defines what your brand is all about. And don't worry if it's not perfect right away, you can always refine it as your business grows. But having that one-sentence summary will give you a solid foundation to build your brand around.

Keep It Real

When building your brand, the most important thing you can do is be authentic and true to yourself. People can sniff out fake branding from a mile away, and they don't like it. So, instead of trying to be something you're not, lean into what makes you and your business unique.

Are you funny, high energy, or super down-to-earth? Let that shine through in your branding. Authenticity resonates, and when customers feel like they're dealing with a real person (or a real company with real values), they're more likely to stick around.

Now that you understand the basics of branding, let's dive into how you can build a standout brand without spending a fortune. You don't need a multi-million-dollar ad campaign to make an impression, you just need some creativity, consistency, and a little elbow grease!

Affordable Branding Hacks

When you're just starting out, your budget is probably closer to "ramen noodles" than "filet mignon," but that doesn't mean your brand has to look cheap. In fact, with a little creativity and a few smart moves, you can create a polished, professional brand image without spending a fortune.

You don't need a marketing team, a branding agency, or a fancy photoshoot to make your side hustle shine. What you do need are some affordable tools and a bit of DIY spirit.

Branding on a Budget

Here are some budget-friendly hacks that will help you get your brand off the ground without breaking the bank:

1. **DIY Logos with Free Tools**: Don't worry if you're not a graphic designer; there are tons of free and low-cost tools out there to help you create a killer logo. Websites like **Canva, Envato** and **Fiverr** allow you to design professional logos with easy drag-and-drop templates. They're super user-friendly, even if your only design experience is choosing a filter for your Instagram photos. Just make sure your logo is clean, simple, and reflects the vibe of your business.

2. **Keep Your Brand Colors and Fonts Consistent**: Consistency is key to a professional look. You don't need to hire a branding expert to pick your colors and fonts, just choose 2-3 colors that reflect the personality of your brand and stick with them. Use these same colors across all your marketing materials, from your website to your social media accounts. Canva also has a free color palette generator if you're stuck. As for fonts, Google Fonts offers free, stylish font options that you can use to create a cohesive feel.

3. **Website on Shoestring**: You can set up a simple, professional-looking website for next to nothing these days. You can try platforms like **GoDaddy**, **WordPress** or **Wix** that offer free templates that can be customized to suit your brand. You don't need to splurge on a custom-built site at the beginning. Just pick a clean design, add your logo, colors, and some clear copy, and voilà, you've got a home for your brand on the internet.

4. **DIY Photography**: Great visuals can make or break your brand, but that doesn't mean you need to hire a professional photographer for every shot. If you have a decent smartphone camera, that's all you need. With natural light, a clean background, and a few helpful YouTube tutorials, you can take some snazzy product or lifestyle photos yourself. You can also use free photo editing tools like **Snapseed** or **Pixlr** to polish them up.

Exercise: Choose Your Business Name and Create a Logo

Time to put these hacks into action! Grab that notebook and let's go:

> **Choose Your Business Name**: Think about what your business represents, and make sure the name reflects that. Write down a few options and say them out loud. Does it sound good? Is it easy to remember? Bonus points if it's available as a domain name (check that on sites like Namecheap or GoDaddy).

> **Create Your Logo**: Head over to Canva or Looka and start playing around with their logo templates. Choose colors that reflect your business's vibe and pick a font that's easy to read. Don't stress about it being perfect, remember, you can always tweak it later. For now, focus on something clean and simple that represents your brand.

By the end of this exercise, you should have a name and a logo for your business, and you don't have to spend a dime! See? Branding on a budget isn't just possible, it's fun! Keep things simple, consistent, and true to your vision, and your brand will look polished, even if your budget isn't.

Building Your Online Presence

Alright, you've got your brand basics down, a name, a logo, and a sense of what you're all about. Now it's time to take things digital because in today's world, **if you're not online, you're basically invisible**. Your online presence is how people find you, learn about your business, and (hopefully) fall in love with what you're offering. Setting up your online presence doesn't have to be complicated or costly. It's all about keeping things simple and focusing on what really matters: connecting with your audience.

Why You Need an Online Presence

Your website and social media profiles are like your digital business card, storefront, and sales team all rolled into one. When someone hears about your business, what's the first thing they're going to do? Google you, of course!

If they can't find you online, or if your website looks like it hasn't been updated since 1999, they might hesitate to trust your business. A polished online presence gives your brand credibility and makes it easier for potential customers to discover what you're all about.

Keep It Simple

You don't need to overthink this. Start with the basics, and you can always refine things later.

1. **Set Up a Simple Website**: Your website doesn't need to be fancy or expensive. Use platforms like **GoDaddy**, **WordPress**, **Wix**, or **Squarespace** to create a clean, easy-to-navigate website. Make sure it includes the essentials: who you are, what you offer, and how people can contact you. Remember, you're not building the Taj Mahal here, just a simple, functional site that lets people learn about your business.

2. **Create Social Media Profiles**: Choose one or two social media platforms where your audience is likely to hang out. For example, if your business is visually appealing (like a cooking or a graphic design service), **Instagram** is a great place to start. If you're targeting professionals,

LinkedIn might be your go-to. Don't try to be everywhere at once, just focus on the platforms that make the most sense for your business. No more than two. I mean that!

Exercise: Build Your Online Presence

It's time to get your online presence up and running! Here's your task:

1. **Create Your First Social Media Profile**: Pick a platform (Instagram, Facebook, LinkedIn, etc.), upload your logo, and fill out the basic information about your business. Write a short, engaging bio that explains what you do and how you help your customers. Don't worry if it's not perfect, just get something up there that reflects your brand's personality.

2. **Draft Your "About" Page**: Open that notebook and write a rough draft of your website's "About" page. Here are a few questions to guide you:
   - Who are you?
   - What does your business do?
   - What makes your business unique?

    o   What's your mission or purpose?

Keep it conversational, like you're talking directly to your ideal customer. This is your chance to tell your story and let people connect with the heart of your business.

Now that your brand is coming together and you've established your online presence, it's time to shift gears and start getting the word out!

THE 7-DAY ENTREPRENEUR

Chapter 5

Marketing That Works (Day 5)

Marketing on a Shoestring Budget

So, you've got your brand in place, your online presence is up, and now it's time for the million-dollar question: **how do you get customers without spending a million dollars?** The good news is you don't need a huge marketing budget to get the word out about your new business. In fact, with a little creativity and some hustle, you can market your business effectively on a shoestring budget.

The Magic of Low-Cost Marketing

When I was starting out, I didn't exactly have a budget for big marketing campaigns. Actually, I didn't have much of a budget at all, just a little cash, a lot of ideas, and that proverbial good cup of coffee!

But what I lacked in funds, I made up for in resourcefulness, and you can do the same.

Here are some low-cost marketing strategies that pack a punch without breaking the bank:

➢ **Leverage Social Media**: Social media is a goldmine for entrepreneurs on a budget. It's free to set up profiles, and you can reach your audience directly.

Focus on creating engaging, shareable content that shows off your brand's personality. Remember, don't worry about being on *every* platform, choose one or two where your target audience hangs out. People love feeling like they're part of something exclusive.

➢ **Content Marketing**: One of the best ways to attract customers without spending a dime is through content marketing. Whether it's blog posts, videos, or even podcasts, share your knowledge and expertise. This not only establishes you as an authority in your niche but also helps you connect with your audience.

Plus, content has a long shelf life, it keeps working for you long after you hit "publish." I've had blog posts bring in clients years after they were written.

Keep It Fun and Authentic

The trick with low-cost marketing is to keep it fun, authentic, and true to your brand. Don't worry about being overly polished, people appreciate realness, and they can spot inauthenticity from a mile away. So, focus on creating content that feels like *you*.

If you've got a quirky sense of humor, let it shine. If you're passionate about what you do, show that enthusiasm. At the end of the day, people don't just buy products or services, they buy into the personality and mission of your brand.

Exercise: Choose Your Top 2 Marketing Channels

Time to get practical! Grab your notebook and write down the top two marketing channels you're going to focus on. Here are some ideas to help you decide:

> ➤ **Social Media**: Which platforms will you use to reach your target audience?
> ➤ **Content Marketing**: Will you start a blog, YouTube channel, or podcast to share your expertise?
> ➤ **Referrals & Word of Mouth**: How will you encourage happy customers to spread the word?

By narrowing it down to just two channels, you can focus your energy where it matters most, and start building momentum without burning through your budget.

Building a Simple Marketing Plan

You've got your budget-friendly marketing strategies in hand, now let's put them into action with a **simple, no-stress marketing plan**. Don't worry, we're not about to create some complicated, 50-page document with fancy charts.

Your marketing plan is just a roadmap that outlines what you're going to do to get your business out there and how often you'll do it. The goal is to create a plan that's easy to follow, realistic, and, most importantly, doable.

Step 1: Set Your Goals

First things first: What are you trying to achieve with your marketing? Maybe you want to gain 100 new followers on social media, drive more traffic to your website, or get five new clients by the end of the month. Whatever your goals are, make sure they're **specific and measurable**. For example:

> ➤ "I want to gain 100 new followers on Instagram this month."
>
> ➤ "I want to book 5 new clients for my design business by the end of the month."
>
> ➤ "I want to drive 200 visitors to my website this month."

These clear goals will help you stay focused and give you something to aim for.

Step 2: Choose Your Content Types

Next, figure out what kind of content you'll create. You don't need to post something new every day or produce hours of video content, keep it simple. Think about what you're comfortable with and what's manageable for you and your lifestyle. Here are a few easy content ideas:

- ➢ **Social Media Posts**: Share a mix of behind-the-scenes content, tips related to your niche, customer testimonials, or product highlights.
- ➢ **Blog Posts**: If you enjoy writing, aim for one blog post a week about topics your customers care about.

- ➢ **Videos or Reels**: Create short, fun videos or Instagram Reels that showcase your products or services. Don't stress about production value, people love authenticity!

- ➢ **Email Newsletters**: If you've started building an email list, send out a simple monthly update or special offers.

For example, if you to start a BBQ rub side hustle, your marketing plan might include posting two Instagram photos of your latest recipe each week, sharing that recipe on your blog, and sending out a newsletter with a special discount to purchase your product(s).

Step 3: Plan Your Content

Now, it's time to organize everything into a manageable schedule. You don't need to be a content machine, just stick to a consistent plan. If you can commit to posting twice a week on social media and writing one blog post a month, that's perfect. The key is to keep it realistic and avoid burning out.

Exercise: Create A One-Month Marketing Calendar

Here's a simple exercise to keep you on track:

- ➤ **Grab a Calendar**: You can use a physical calendar, Google Calendar, or even just a notebook.

- ➤ **Write Down Your Content Ideas**: For each week, write down what content you'll post and on which platform. Keep it simple, like:
    - ○ **Week 1:** Post a behind-the-scenes Facebook/Instagram story, share a blog post about common mistakes in your industry.

- o **Week 2:** Post a customer testimonial on Facebook, share a Reel about your product or service.
- o **Week 3:** Post a fun "day in the life" photo on Instagram, send out an email with a limited-time offer.
- o **Week 4:** Post a tip related to your industry, host a quick Instagram Live Q&A.

- ➤ **Set Realistic Goals**: Decide how many times you'll post each week and set small, achievable goals. Maybe you want to post on Instagram twice a week, send out one email, and create a blog post. That's it!

By creating a simple marketing calendar, you'll have a clear plan in place that takes the guesswork out of your marketing efforts. Plus, this method helps you stay consistent without overwhelming yourself.

With your marketing plan in place, you're ready to start building momentum! But marketing isn't just about creating content, it's also about building relationships.

Effective Networking

Just the word "networking" can make some people feel stressed and overwhelmed. Images of awkward cocktail hours and giving your elevator pitches to complete strangers might come to mind, but the truth is that **networking doesn't have to be difficult**. In fact, it can be one of the most genuine and powerful ways to grow your business. It's not about handing out business cards like candy or trying to impress people with your sales pitch. Networking is about building real relationships that can lead to amazing opportunities, often when you least expect it.

The Power of Networking

People do business with people they like and trust. That's why networking is so important. When you genuinely connect with someone, you're not just another name in their inbox; you're someone they'll think of when they need what you offer.

Whether it's other entrepreneurs, potential clients, or industry influencers, those relationships can open doors you didn't even know existed.

One of my biggest business opportunities came from a casual conversation at a local event. I wasn't trying to pitch my business; I was just chatting with someone about our mutual love for travel. Turns out, they worked in an industry I'd been hoping to break into as a speaker. One thing led to another, and before I knew it, I had a partnership that took me across the pond to the United Kingdom at least 10 times, with a large amount of revenue being made each time. I didn't treat the initial conversation like a transaction, I treated it like a chance to connect, and it paid off in ways I never could have planned.

How to Network Like a Pro

So, how do you network without feeling like a used car salesman? Simple: **be yourself**. Focus on building genuine relationships rather than trying to "sell" yourself. Ask questions, listen, and offer help where you can. The best networking happens when there's mutual respect and interest, not when you're trying to push your agenda.

Exercise: Build Your Network

Grab your notebook and list three people in your industry you'd like to connect with. These could be fellow entrepreneurs, potential clients, or even people you admire. Once you have your list, reach out! It could be a casual message on LinkedIn, an email introduction, or even a coffee meetup (virtual or in-person). Remember, the goal is to build a relationship, not to make an immediate sale. Be genuine, and opportunities will naturally follow.

Now that you've got your marketing plan and networking strategy in place, you're on your way to building a strong, connected business.

THE 7-DAY ENTREPRENEUR

Chapter 6

Money, Money, Money (Day 6)

Pricing for Profit

It's time to talk about something that makes a lot of new entrepreneurs break into a nervous sweat: **pricing**. How much do you charge for your product or service? Too high, and you risk scaring off potential customers. Too low, and you might as well be paying them to take your product. But here's the thing: **pricing shouldn't be a guessing game**. It's all about knowing your worth and charging accordingly.

The Biggest Pricing Mistake: Undervaluing Yourself
One of the most common mistakes that I see new entrepreneurs make is **undervaluing their products or services**. It's easy to fall into the trap of

thinking, "If I charge less, I'll attract more customers!" But here's the cold, hard truth: **low prices don't always equal more business**. In fact, undervaluing yourself can send the wrong message, it makes people think your product or service is lower quality or that you're not confident in what you're offering.

How to Set Prices Confidently

Here are a few straightforward steps to set prices that reflect the value you're offering:

> - **Know Your Costs**: Start by calculating how much it costs to create your product or deliver your service. This includes materials, time, and any overhead (like website fees, shipping costs, or tools). Once you know your costs, you'll have a baseline to ensure you're not losing money.

> - **Research the Market**: Look at what others in your niche are charging. This will give you an idea of the going rate and where your pricing can fit in. Don't aim to be the cheapest, aim to be competitive *and* valuable.

> **Factor in Your Time**: Your time is one of your most valuable resources. Make sure you're paying yourself fairly. If it takes you 10 hours to complete a project, but you're only charging $100, well, you're earning less than minimum wage. That's a fast track to burnout and failure.

> **Add a Profit Margin**: Once you've covered your costs, it's time to add a profit margin. This is the extra amount that ensures you're not just breaking even but making a profit. A good rule of thumb is to aim for a margin that allows for growth and reinvestment in your business.

Exercise: Set Your Initial Pricing Strategy

Now it's your turn to set prices confidently. Grab your notebook and work through these steps:

> **List Your Costs**: Write down all the costs associated with producing your product or offering your service. Include both materials and your time.

> **Research Competitor Pricing**: Look at 3-5 competitors in your niche. What are they

charging? Are their products or services similar to yours? Use this as a reference point.

➢ **Determine Your Profit Margin**: Decide how much profit you want to make on each sale. Don't be afraid to aim for a margin that reflects the value you bring.

By the end of this exercise, you should have a clear pricing strategy that ensures you're covering costs, paying yourself fairly, and making a profit. Remember, **don't undervalue yourself**, you're offering something valuable, and you deserve to be compensated accordingly.

Budgeting Basics

Alright, you've got your pricing sorted, so now let's talk about **budgeting**. I know, budgeting doesn't exactly scream "fun," but trust me, it's essential for making sure your side hustle isn't just bringing in money, but also keeping it. Think of a budget as your financial roadmap, it shows you where your money is going and helps you stay in control of your finances. Plus, it takes the guesswork out of decision-making when it comes to spending.

Why Budgeting Matters

Whether you're selling handcrafted jewelry or offering virtual fitness classes, your business will have costs. Some are obvious, like materials or website fees, while others, like taxes or software subscriptions, might sneak up on you. **Without a budget, it's easy to overspend without even realizing it**. But with a solid budget in place, you'll know exactly how much you're spending, how much you're earning, and how much profit you're actually making.

Think of it this way: you wouldn't bake a cake without knowing how much flour, sugar, and butter to use, right? The same goes for your finances. A budget gives you the recipe for success, helping you mix the right amounts of spending, saving, and investing to keep your business growing.

How to Set Up a Simple Budget

You don't need a fancy accounting degree to set up a budget. Here's a straightforward method you can follow to get started:

1. **Track Your Income**: First things first, write down all the money you're bringing in. This includes sales, service fees, or any other revenue streams. Be honest with yourself, don't include money you *expect* to make, just what's actually coming in right now.

2. **List Your Expenses**: Next, list all the expenses related to your side hustle. This can include things like:
   o   Materials or products
   o   Website hosting fees
   o   Shipping costs
   o   Advertising or marketing costs
   o   Software or tools
   o   Taxes (yes, you'll need to plan for those too!)

3. **Divide Your Expenses into Fixed and Variable Costs**: Fixed costs stay the same each month (like website fees), while variable costs can change (like materials or shipping). This will help you plan for expenses that fluctuate.

4. **Calculate Your Profit**: Subtract your total expenses from your total income. This is your profit, aka the money you get to keep. If you find you're barely breaking even, it might be time to adjust your pricing or cut down on unnecessary expenses.

5. **Set Spending Goals**: Now that you know where your money is going, set some spending limits for yourself. How much can you afford to spend on marketing each month? How much do you need to set aside for taxes or reinvestment in your business?

Exercise: Create Your Side Hustle Budget

Now it's your turn! Grab your notebook and create a simple budget for your side hustle:

➢ **List Your Monthly Income**: Write down how much money you're making each month from your side hustle.

➢ **List Your Monthly Expenses**: Break these into fixed and variable costs. Be sure to include everything, from materials to marketing.

> ➤ **Calculate Your Profit**: Subtract your total expenses from your income. This is the amount you'll be taking home (or reinvesting in your business).

By the end of this exercise, you'll have a clear picture of your business finances. A budget isn't just about keeping costs under control, it's about making sure your side hustle stays profitable and sustainable in the long run.

If your side hustle doesn't make any money, it's called a HOBBY!

And remember, **a budget is a living document**. Update it regularly as your business grows and your expenses change.

Now that you've got a handle on budgeting, you're well on your way to financial success. But there's still one more thing we need to cover: how to scale your side hustle for growth.

Scaling Without Stressing

Once your side hustle is making money and you've got a budget in place, you might start thinking about **scaling**, depending on the lifestyle choices you have made. If you are simply looking for some extra income for your summer vacation, scaling will be a relative term. Not everyone wants to grow their business into a 3-headed monster complete with employees and lots of overhead. You need to keep this in mind when considering the topic of scaling your side hustle.

Scaling doesn't have to mean stressing. You can absolutely grow your business without overwhelming yourself or losing that balance between work and life. In fact, growing smart is the key to keeping your side hustle fun, manageable, and sustainable.

Scaling Step by Step

You don't need to scale your business overnight. Growth should happen **step by step**, so you don't end up working 80 hours a week and hating every minute of it. The goal here is to grow in a way that aligns with your lifestyle and the amount of time you want to dedicate to your business.

Several years ago, I was scaling one of my businesses, I made the mistake of saying "yes" to everything that came my way. More clients, more projects, more work, it sounded great at first. It was a limousines business, and I started out with a single limousine so that I could take my family out for our "Friday Night Date Nights." So, I hired a chauffer and away I went.

But pretty soon, I was juggling so much that I felt like I was running a three-ring circus. Because I know how to get customers pretty easily to any business I have, we went from zero revenue to over $1,000,000 within 1 years. We also went from that single limo to an entire fleet of limos, plus a large Party Bus. I was working around the clock, and let's just say my stress levels were through the roof. We would take on any new client or opportunity that came our way.

Eventually, I realized that **growth doesn't mean taking on everything**, it means being strategic about what's truly going to help you grow *without* burning out.

Just at the right time, a buyer came along and I sold them to basket of headaches!

How to Scale Smart

Here are a few practical tips to help you scale your business without losing your mind:

- ➢ **Automate Where You Can**: One of the best ways to grow without adding more hours to your day is to automate repetitive tasks. Use tools like email marketing automation, scheduling apps, or even chatbots to handle some of the day-to-day stuff that eats up your time.

- ➢ **Outsource Tasks**: You don't have to do everything yourself. Once you have a bit of profit, consider outsourcing tasks that are time-consuming or outside your expertise. Whether it's hiring a virtual assistant to manage your admin work or bringing on a freelance designer to help with branding, outsourcing can free up your time to focus on scaling.

> **Focus on What Works**: Don't feel like you need to expand into a bunch of new areas just because you're growing. Instead, focus on what's already working and double down on that. If social media is bringing in clients, put more energy into it. If your product is selling well in one market, see how you can expand into similar markets. Growth doesn't mean reinventing the wheel, it means fine-tuning and expanding what's already successful.

Exercise: Brainstorm Your Scaling Ideas

Take a moment to brainstorm two ways you could scale your business when the time is right. Here are some ideas to get you started:

- **Expand Your Offerings**: Could you introduce a new product or service that complements what you're already offering?

- **Increase Your Reach**: Is there a new market or customer base you could tap into? Could you sell your products online if you're not already doing so?

Write these ideas down in your notebook and keep them in mind as your business grows. Scaling doesn't have to be stressful, as long as you do it on your own terms.

Chapter 7

The Hustle & Flow (Day 7)

Work Smarter, Not Harder

Here we are—**Day 7**! You've made it to the final stretch, and now it's time to talk about something I live by: **working smarter, not harder**. It's a phrase you've probably heard a million times, but trust me, it's more than just a catchy slogan, it's a way of life.

If you've been thinking that building a successful side hustle means working non-stop until you collapse in a heap of exhaustion, I'm here to tell you there's a better way.

The goal isn't to grind yourself into the ground, **the goal is to create a business that fits your**

lifestyle, not the other way around. You started this side hustle because you wanted more time freedom, financial freedom, flexibility, or fulfillment. But what good is it if you're working 24/7 and can't enjoy the benefits? That's where working smarter comes in. It's about finding ways to be efficient, productive, and focused so you can get more done in less time and still have space for the things that matter most.

The Magic of Working Smarter

I've been a lifestyle entrepreneur for over 35 years, and let me tell you, one of the best decisions I ever made was deciding to live by the NEW 24/7 MENTALITY... **24 hours a week, 7 months a year**. No, I'm not some wizard with magical productivity powers, I just realized early on that my time is my most valuable resource. Instead of working more, I focused on working better. That meant cutting out distractions, automating repetitive tasks, and learning when to say "no" to things that didn't align with my goals.

Here's the kicker: **you don't have to work harder to be successful**. You just need to be intentional about how you spend your time. That means prioritizing the tasks that move the needle in your business and letting go of the busywork that makes you *feel* productive but doesn't actually contribute to your growth.

Balance is Key

The key to working smarter is balance. Yes, your side hustle is important, but so is your personal life. The trick is finding the sweet spot where your business and life can coexist without one overwhelming the other. That might mean setting strict boundaries around your work hours or learning to delegate tasks as your business grows.

I get it, when you're passionate about your business, it's easy to get carried away and spend all your free time hustling. But burnout is real, and trust me, you don't want to get there. A balanced approach to your side hustle not only keeps you energized and motivated, but it also makes your work more enjoyable in the long run.

Exercise: Create Your Time Management Plan

It's time to put this "work smarter, not harder" philosophy into practice. Grab your notebook, and let's create a simple time management plan that helps you balance your side hustle and personal life:

85

> **Set Your Work Hours**: Decide how many hours you want to dedicate to your side hustle each week. Be realistic, this isn't about working every spare second, but finding a schedule that fits your life. Maybe it's two hours a day or weekends only. The key is to **set boundaries**.

> **Prioritize Your Tasks**: Write down your top 3 business priorities for the week. What are the most important tasks that will move your business forward? Focus on these first, and let go of the little things that can wait.

> **Schedule Breaks & Personal Time**: Block out time for yourself, whether it's spending time with family, exercising, or just relaxing. **You're not a robot**, and you need time to recharge.

By the end of this exercise, you'll have a clear, balanced schedule that allows you to hustle without losing sight of what really matters, your well-being.

Now that you've got your time management plan in place, you're well on your way to creating a business that fits your lifestyle. But there's more to balance than just scheduling your work, there's also the art of staying motivated and handling setbacks.

Staying Motivated and Avoiding Burnout

Let's face it, no matter how passionate you are about your side hustle, there are going to be days when your motivation tank is running on empty. Maybe a project didn't go as planned, or you've just been burning the candle at both ends for too long. **Burnout** is a real risk for any entrepreneur, especially when you're trying to balance your side hustle with the rest of your life. But here's the good news: you don't have to let burnout sneak up on you, and with a few simple strategies, you can stay motivated even during the tough times.

Keep the Spark Alive

Motivation doesn't always come naturally, and that's okay. **The key is knowing how to reignite that spark when it starts to flicker.** One of the best ways to stay motivated is to remind yourself why you started this journey in the first place. Remember your "why"? Whether it's financial freedom, time freedom, following a passion, or building something for your future, keeping your core motivation front and center can help you push through the rough patches.

It's also important to mix things up. Sometimes, doing the same routine day after day can lead to burnout. If you're feeling stuck, try switching gears. Tackle a new project, brainstorm fresh ideas, or even take a day off to recharge. Giving yourself permission to step away can be one of the best ways to come back feeling re-energized and ready to roll.

My Slump Story

Let me tell you about a time when I hit a serious motivation slump. One of my businesses was going through a slow period, and nothing seemed to be working. Sales were down, I was stressed, and my usual go-getter attitude felt more like a "maybe later" kind of vibe. I was tempted to throw in the towel and take a long nap.

But here's what saved me: **I focused on small wins.** Instead of stressing about the big picture, I started celebrating little victories, like landing one new client or completing a project ahead of schedule. Focusing on those smaller achievements helped me build momentum, and before I knew it, I was back on track, feeling motivated and energized.

Sometimes, motivation comes from taking a step back and recognizing that progress isn't always linear. Even on tough days, you're still moving forward, and that's something to be proud of.

Avoiding Burnout

To avoid burnout, **self-care is non-negotiable**. You can't pour from an empty cup, so make sure you're taking time to rest, recharge, and do things that make you happy outside of your hustle. Whether it's going for a walk, spending time with friends, or binge-watching your favorite show, don't feel guilty about taking time for yourself. Your business will thank you for it.

Exercise: Energize Your Hustle

Let's get practical; Write down 3 things you'll do to stay motivated and energized when times get tough. Here are a few ideas to get you started:

1. **Take Breaks**: Schedule regular breaks to avoid burnout. Even a 10-minute walk outside can help you reset.

2. **Celebrate Small Wins**: Make a habit of celebrating your progress, no matter how small.

3. **Reconnect with Your "Why"**: When motivation fades, remind yourself of the bigger picture and why you started this journey in the first place.

By the end of this exercise, you'll have a go-to list of strategies to keep your hustle going strong, even when the going gets tough.

Now that you've got strategies for staying motivated and avoiding burnout, it's time to bring everything together. You've put in the work, and now it's time to reflect on how far you've come and where you're headed next.

Setting Goals and Celebrating Wins

You've made it through seven days of entrepreneurial bootcamp, and now it's time to focus on something that's just as important as hustling: **celebrating your wins**! Setting goals and acknowledging your achievements isn't just about checking things off a list, it's about reminding yourself of the progress you've made, no matter how big or small. **The journey is just as important as the destination**, and every milestone is worth celebrating.

Setting Achievable Goals

When it comes to setting goals, the key is to make them **achievable**. Sure, it's great to have big dreams, but breaking them down into smaller, bite-sized goals makes the journey feel less overwhelming and more doable. Think of it as building a staircase, each small step you take gets you closer to the top. Plus, reaching those smaller goals gives you a sense of accomplishment and momentum, which keeps you motivated to keep going.

For example, instead of setting a goal like, "Make a million dollars by next year", start with, "Land five new clients in the next two months," or, "Double my website traffic by the end of the quarter." These smaller, concrete goals will help you stay focused and make consistent progress.

Celebrate Your Wins

Now, let's talk about something that a lot of entrepreneurs forget to do: **celebrating your wins**! It's easy to get caught up in the hustle and move straight from one goal to the next without taking a moment to reflect and celebrate. But you deserve to recognize the hard work you've put in. Whether it's a small victory like launching your website or a major win like hitting a sales target, take the time to celebrate, you've earned it!

And don't think celebrations have to be extravagant! Maybe it's a dinner out, a weekend off, or even just treating yourself to your favorite dessert. The point is to acknowledge your progress and enjoy the fruits of your labor. This isn't just about boosting morale; celebrating your wins keeps the journey fun and sustainable.

Exercise: Milestones & Rewards

Grab your notebook and take a moment to write down a few milestones you want to hit over the next few months. These could be:

> ➢ Reaching a certain number of clients
> ➢ Launching a new product or service
> ➢ Hitting a sales goal
> ➢ Expanding your audience on social media

Next, write down a reward for each milestone. Think of things that will make you feel good and keep you motivated, like:

> ➢ Taking a day off to recharge
> ➢ Splurging on something you've had your eye on
> ➢ Treating yourself to a fun experience, like a spa day or a mini-vacation

By the end of this exercise, you'll have a roadmap of goals to keep you on track, and plenty of reasons to celebrate along the way!

As you wrap up this 7-day game plan, take a moment to reflect on how far you've come. You've laid the foundation for something amazing, and the journey is just getting started. In **conclusion**, we'll tie everything together and get you pumped up for the next steps in your entrepreneurial adventure.

THE 7-DAY ENTREPRENEUR

Conclusion

Your Entrepreneurial Journey Begins Now

You did it! You've made it through the 7-day entrepreneurial boot camp, and now you're standing at the start of something exciting, **your very own entrepreneurial journey**. Whether you're building your business on the side or preparing to make it your full-time gig, you've laid the foundation to turn your idea into something real.

You've tackled the essentials, from shaping the right mindset to creating a simple MVP, and you've learned how to market yourself without spending a fortune. Now, it's time to take everything you've learned and **put it into action**.

Recap of Your 7-Day Journey

Let's take a quick look back at everything you've accomplished in just seven days:

> ➤ On **Day 1**, you developed the **entrepreneurial mindset**, busting myths about who can be an entrepreneur and defining your "why." You learned that anyone can build something great with the right attitude and resilience.

> ➤ On **Day 2**, you tapped into your passions and found your niche. You identified what excites you and discovered how to turn that into a profitable side hustle.

> ➤ **Day 3** was all about creating your **Minimum Viable Product**, the simplest version of your offering that solves a problem and allows you to gather feedback. You learned that starting small and scaling is the key to success.

> ➤ **Day 4** taught you how to **build a brand on a budget**. From crafting your logo to setting up

your online presence, you created a brand that resonates with your target audience.

> On **Day 5**, you created a **marketing plan** that works without blowing your budget. You learned how to market your business strategically and build relationships that fuel your growth.

> On **Day 6**, you tackled the world of money, **pricing your products for profit** and setting up a budget to keep your business running smoothly. You also learned how to scale without stressing yourself out.

> Finally, on **Day 7**, you focused on finding balance, staying motivated, and celebrating your wins. You created a time management plan that works for you, and you set goals that will keep you moving forward.

That's a lot to cover in just a week, but you did it! You've built a strong foundation for your business, and now the real adventure begins.

Take Immediate Action

Here's the most important thing: **don't stop now**. The biggest mistake new entrepreneurs make is waiting for the "perfect" time to start. They think they need more preparation, more research, more time. But guess what? There's no perfect time. You've got everything you need right now to take the first step, and you can learn, grow, and adjust along the way.

Every successful entrepreneur started where you are now, with an idea and a whole lot of questions. But what sets them apart is that they took action, even when they didn't have all the answers. So, whether you're launching your MVP, setting up your website, or sending that first marketing email, **do something today**! Keep moving forward, even if it's a small step. Those small actions will add up faster than you think.

A Final Story

Let me tell you one last story before you dive into your own journey. When I first started out as an entrepreneur, I didn't have it all figured out. I suffered lots of failure along the way that could have taken the umph right out of me. But I didn't give up. One of my businesses, one that I thought was going to be the "next big thing", completely flopped. I had put in countless hours, stressed over every detail, and when it failed, I was devastated.

But here's what I learned: **failure isn't the end—it's a stepping stone**. That flop taught me valuable lessons about what to do differently next time, and it eventually led to the success with my next idea. If I had given up after that first failure, I wouldn't be here today, sharing this journey with you.

My point is, don't be afraid to stumble. Don't let fear of failure hold you back. Every mistake is a lesson, and every lesson brings you closer to success.

Keep Learning, Growing, and Adjusting

Entrepreneurship isn't a one-and-done deal, it's a journey. You'll continue to learn, grow, and adjust as you go, and that's the beauty of it. There are days when everything feels like it's clicking, and days when you wonder if you're on the right path. But as long as you keep moving forward, you'll keep progressing.

Celebrate every win, no matter how small. Take time to reflect on your progress and reset when you need to. Keep connecting with others, learning new skills, and adapting to new challenges. The more you grow as an entrepreneur, the more your business will grow with you.

Final Call to Action

Your entrepreneurial journey begins now. You have the tools, the mindset, and the plan to make your side hustle a reality. Go out there, take action, and watch your business grow. And remember, you're not alone in this. Keep pushing forward, keep learning, and most importantly, keep believing in yourself.

This is just the beginning. **You've got this.**

BONUS CHAPTERS

The 15 Top Ways to Start a Side Hustle Business This Year

A DIY Guide for the Aspiring Couch CEOs

Bonus Chapter 1:

Welcome to Your Living Room, Inc.

Back in the not-too-distant pass, flying cars were going to be the transportation of the future. If I'm correct, they have been talking about flying cars for many decades. Well, maybe flying cars aren't coming our way any time soon, but starting a business from the comfort of your own home certainly is. Forget the daunting skyscrapers and stuffy suits; your next business venture can be launched between your first cup of coffee and your last bite of breakfast cereal. Here are the top 15 ways to turn your domicile into your empire's headquarters.

1. Freelance Like You Mean It

The gig economy isn't just surviving; it's thriving. Websites like Upwork, Freelancer, and Fiverr can help you turn your skills into bills. Whether you're a graphic designer, writer, software developer, or a consultant, there's a gig waiting for your bid. **Steps to Launch:**

- Identify your marketable skills.

- Set up a winning profile on several freelance platforms.

- Start with competitive pricing, gather reviews, then gradually increase your rates.

2. Craft Your Way to Success

Etsy isn't just for knitted hats and homemade candles anymore. It's a global marketplace for anything unique. If you can make it, you can sell it. **Steps to Launch:**

- Pick your craft or product.

- Create a brand that tells your artisan story.

- Set up an Etsy shop with high-quality photos and SEO-friendly descriptions.

3. Consulting from the Couch

Use that dusty degree or your industry experience by consulting from home. Companies pay top dollar for expert advice on everything from HR policies to IT setups. **Steps to Launch:**

- Define your niche based on expertise.

- Build a simple website outlining your services.

- Network online and offline—sometimes your next big client could be your former employer.

4. Home-Based Bakery or Food Business

Turn your kitchen into a culinary workshop. Thanks to apps like UberEats and DoorDash, your home can be the next culinary hotspot. **Steps to Launch:**

- Check local regulations and obtain necessary permits.

- Define your menu. Start small but delicious.

- Use social media to tempt local taste buds with your dishes.

5. Online Tutoring or Courses

If you know things, teach them. The world is always looking for knowledge, especially in an era where parents will pay premiums for their kids to learn quantum physics from a friendly face online. **Steps to Launch:**

- Choose your subject and prepare course materials.

- Sign up on platforms like Tutor.com or create courses on Udemy.

- Promote your courses through social media and content marketing.

6. YouTube Stardom

Got a charismatic personality or a quirky talent? Maybe it's time to broadcast it to the world. **Steps to Launch:**

- Choose your niche: unboxings, reviews, tutorials, or daily vlogs.

- Consistently create and upload high-quality videos.

- Engage with your viewers and monetize through ads, sponsorships, and merchandise.

7. Fitness Guru

Turn your passion for fitness into a profitable venture from your home gym or living room. **Steps to Launch:**

- Get certified as a personal trainer.

- Create workout plans or video classes.

- Market through social media and fitness apps.

8. Graphic Design Studio

Branding, website design, posters—you name it. If you can imagine it, you can design it. **Steps to Launch:**

- Build a compelling portfolio.

- Network on LinkedIn and Instagram.

- Offer your services on design-specific platforms like 99Designs.

9. Virtual Assistant

Help others manage their schedules, emails, and lives from your dining table. **Steps to Launch:**

- List the services you can offer, such as email management, scheduling, or content preparation.

- Set up a professional website or profile on platforms like Belay.

- Start small with one or two clients, and as you become more efficient, scale up.

10. Tech Support

Offer support for software, hardware, or networks to individuals and small businesses. **Steps to Launch:**

- Verify your IT credentials and skills.

- Decide whether to offer local in-home support, remote support, or both.

- Market to local businesses and neighborhoods.

11. Professional Blogger

Turn your insights, hobbies, or experiences into engaging blog posts that can attract ads, sponsorships, or affiliate marketing revenues. **Steps to Launch:**

- Identify your niche and target audience.

- Set up a blog with a reputable CMS like WordPress.

- Consistently produce valuable and SEO-optimized content to build your audience.

12. Real Estate Investor

Even if you're not ready to buy properties, you can start a business managing real estate investments for others. **Steps to Launch:**

- Learn the market by studying successful investors and market trends.

- Start with small investments or partnerships.

- Build a network of potential buyers, sellers, and fellow investors.

13. Subscription Boxes

Curate and send monthly boxes of goodies, whether it's for pet lovers, makeup enthusiasts, or spicy food aficionados. **Steps to Launch:**

- Decide on a niche with a dedicated and passionate audience.

- Source products and design your first box.

- Set up a subscription model and promote on social media.

14. Digital Marketing Agency

Help other businesses get noticed online by offering SEO, PPC, social media marketing, and more. **Steps to Launch:**

- Gain certifications and knowledge in various digital marketing disciplines.

- Build a robust online presence to showcase your capabilities.

- Reach out to small businesses in your network.

15. Art Gallery

Transform your home into a gallery for your or others' artwork, selling pieces both physically and digitally.

Steps to Launch:

- Curate a collection and create an attractive, navigable online gallery.

- Promote through social media, art shows, and community events.

- Connect with local and online art communities to expand your reach.

Ready, Set, Go!

So, there you have it, 15 viable business ideas that could turn your living space into your earning space. Remember, the path from idea to income is rarely a straight line, it's more like a fun, twisty, and utterly unpredictable ride. Embrace it, enjoy it, and who knows? Your home office might just be the birthplace of the next big thing.

Bonus Chapter 2

The Dozen Dreamers: Simple Ideas That Became Game Changers

Sometimes, we need a little spark or kickstart in order to get our creativity flowing. Here is a collection of business ideas that started small and grew into businesses that have made a dent in the business world, and have become mainstays in our mind.

1. The Sweet Success of Chocolate Chip Cookies

Ruth Wakefield, an accomplished chef and savvy businesswoman, didn't just stumble upon the chocolate chip cookie by accident; she refined it through trial and error. After adding chopped up chocolate to her cookie dough and realizing it didn't melt as expected, she saw the potential for something unique. The challenge, however, was convincing others that her accidental recipe was worth trying. By striking a deal with Nestlé, where her recipe would be printed on the packaging of their chocolate bars, she not only secured a supply of chocolate for her creations but also ensured her culinary invention would become a household name. This strategic partnership exemplifies how recognizing and seizing an opportunity can lead to sweet success.

2. A Sticky Situation: Post-it Notes

Spencer Silver developed a unique, repositionable adhesive at 3M, but initially, no viable application for the product was found, rendering it a solution without a problem. Art Fry, his colleague, recognized its potential during a choir practice as a bookmark that wouldn't slip out of his hymnal. The journey from this realization to the actual product launch of Post-it Notes was fraught with skepticism from executives. Fry and Silver had to conduct numerous demonstrations and give out countless samples to prove the product's worth, showcasing persistence in the face of internal doubt.

3. Turning Water into Clean Water: LifeStraw

Torben Vestergaard Frandsen initially developed the LifeStraw for people afflicted by guinea worm disease, but the broader application for general water purification required significant redesign and rethinking marketing strategies. The challenge was not just technical but also educational, as many communities needed convincing that this simple straw could provide immediate health benefits. Frandsen's team spent considerable time conducting field tests and educational programs to demonstrate the product's effectiveness, emphasizing the importance of direct engagement and education in launching a new product.

4. The Magic of Velcro

George de Mestral patented Velcro in 1955 but faced the monumental task of convincing manufacturers that his hook-and-loop fastener was practical and commercially viable. His early prototypes were bulky and unattractive, which did little to persuade potential partners. Through relentless refinement and by showcasing the product's ease of use and versatility, de Mestral finally broke through the market resistance, securing contracts that would eventually lead to Velcro becoming a ubiquitous product used across various industries.

5. Soothing Moves: Spanx

Sara Blakely's journey with Spanx began with a need and a pair of scissors. Transforming her idea into a globally recognized brand required overcoming gender biases in a male-dominated industry. Pitching a women's product to male investors proved challenging, as many failed to see its potential. Sara's relentless pursuit, attending trade shows, cold-calling manufacturers, and personally writing her patent, demonstrated her commitment and slowly but surely garnered the industry respect and consumer trust necessary to build the Spanx empire.

6. From Baby Slings to Millions: The BabyBjörn

Björn Jakobson faced cultural skepticism when introducing BabyBjörn in a market unaccustomed to men carrying babies in slings. His idea required not just creating a comfortable, safe product but also changing societal perceptions about parenting roles. His dedication to safety and ergonomic design, coupled with strategic marketing campaigns targeting both mothers and fathers, gradually shifted public opinion, turning BabyBjörn into a symbol of modern, involved parenting.

7. A Cooler Cooler: The Coolest Cooler

Ryan Grepper's initial Kickstarter campaign failed, teaching him that even a good idea needs great timing and presentation. He refined his product design and relaunched with a more appealing campaign at the start of summer, leading to one of the most successful Kickstarter campaigns ever. This experience underscores the importance of resilience and timing in entrepreneurship.

8. Flipping a Lid: The Mason Jar

John Landis Mason's invention initially failed to make significant commercial impact because he lacked the resources to mass-produce or market it effectively. His patents eventually expired, allowing others to capitalize on the idea. This tale highlights the importance of not only having a great product but also securing the means to protect and promote it.

9. Wheels of Fortune: The Skateboard

The initial creators of the skateboard, often anonymous surfers, didn't profit from their invention. It took business-minded individuals who saw the broader application and commercial potential to turn skateboarding into a cultural phenomenon and profitable industry. This evolution from a backyard pastime to a mainstream sport required vision and an understanding of youth culture.

10. The Slinky: Accidental Genius

Richard James' invention was initially a stabilizing tool for naval equipment before becoming a toy. The transition from prototype to product involved significant risk; using the family's savings, James and his wife bet on its appeal as a Christmas toy. The initial sales at a local department store were slow until they demonstrated the Slinky in action, proving that sometimes, seeing is believing.

11. Taking a Seat: The Bean Bag

The designers of the bean bag, Piero Gatti, Cesare Paolini, and Franco Teodoro, approached furniture design from a non-traditional angle which was initially met with intrigue and skepticism. Convincing a traditional furniture market of the viability of their design required persistence and innovative marketing strategies, including public sit-ins and involvement in avant-garde art installations, to demonstrate the bean bag's versatility and appeal.

12. Pop Culture Icon: The Super Soaker

Lonnie Johnson faced numerous rejections when pitching his high-powered water gun, with many companies unable to see the appeal. He persisted, however, and after securing a contract with Larami Corporation, extensive marketing and branding efforts helped propel the Super Soaker into becoming a staple of summer fun. Johnson's experience exemplifies the need for perseverance and the right partnership in transforming a good idea into a cultural icon.

Each of these stories is not just about a moment of inspiration but a saga of overcoming doubt, setbacks, and often, industry norms. These entrepreneurs teach us that transforming a simple idea into a global phenomenon requires more than just creativity; they demands resilience, adaptability, and the courage to dream big.

Action Steps: Learn from the Dreamers and Turn Your Idea into a Game Changer

You've just seen how some of the world's most successful businesses started from simple ideas in the bonus chapter "The Dozen Dreamers: Simple Ideas That Became Game Changers." Now, it's time to take that inspiration and put it into action. Here are a few steps to help you turn your idea into the next game-changer.

1. Reflect on Your Own Simple Idea

Simple ideas can lead to great success when they solve real problems.

Action: Write down your own simple idea or brainstorm new ones.

Why This Matters: Understanding that even the smallest ideas can grow gives you confidence to move forward.

How to Do It: Think about a common problem or frustration in your life or industry, and how your idea could solve it.

2. Identify the Key Value of Your Idea

What makes your idea valuable to others?

- **Action:** Define the core value your idea provides.
- **Why This Matters:** Knowing your idea's main benefit helps you focus on its potential.
- **How to Do It:** Ask yourself, What problem does this solve? Whether it's saving time, money, or offering convenience, highlight that benefit.

3. Study One of the "Dozen Dreamers" Closely

Learn from those who have already succeeded.

- **Action:** Research one Dreamer from the chapter that inspires you.
- **Why This Matters:** Studying how others succeeded gives you insight and motivation.
- **How to Do It:** Dive deeper into their journey, what did they do right, and what challenges did they overcome?

4. Take One Small Step

Success begins with the first step.

- **Action:** Take one small action toward bringing your idea to life.
- **Why This Matters:** Even a tiny step forward builds momentum.
- **How to Do It:** This could be creating a sketch, talking to someone about your idea, or starting a basic plan.

Keep Dreaming Big, But Start Small

These Dreamers proved that no idea is too small to make a difference. Now it's your turn to take what you've learned from their stories and start applying it to your own entrepreneurial journey. Remember, every game-changer started with a single step, your success story begins with the actions you take today.

Bonus Chapter: 3

Concluding Thoughts - Embarking on Your Entrepreneurial Journey

The Final Pep Talk: Your Entrepreneurial Launchpad

As we close the pages of this whirlwind guide, you stand at the threshold of what could be the most exhilarating adventure of your life. Starting a business is more than just a means to earn a living; it's a way to create, to innovate, and to impact the world in your unique way.

It's about turning the 'what ifs' into 'what is', transforming dreams into tangible realities. If the journey of entrepreneurship were easy, everyone would

125

be doing it. But you, brave soul, have dared to dance with possibility.

The Entrepreneurial Spirit: Embracing the Challenge

Imagine standing at the edge of a vast ocean. Behind you lies the comfort and safety of the familiar; ahead, the mysterious and untamed waters of entrepreneurship. Taking that first step into the unknown requires courage, but it's also where the magic happens. Every great venture starts with the decision to try, to risk, and to step forward despite the fear of failure.

Entrepreneurship is not a path for the faint-hearted. It is a journey replete with challenges and setbacks. But each obstacle is a steppingstone to greater resilience and wisdom. Embrace these challenges as part of your growth, not as signs to turn back. Remember, the most successful entrepreneurs are not those who never fail but those who never quit.

The Power of Vision: Seeing Beyond the Horizon

Your vision for your business is its beating heart. It's what fuels your passion, guides your decisions, and draws others to your cause. A clear, compelling vision acts as a north star, a constant in the chaotic cosmos of business operations. As you move forward, keep this vision crisp and visible. Let it be the light that guides you through uncertainty and the anchor that holds you steady in stormy seas.

A powerful vision also has the unique capacity to inspire and mobilize. It attracts like-minded individuals, employees, partners, investors, who can help magnify your efforts. Share your vision passionately and openly. Let it resonate in every interaction, every product, every marketing message. When people see the authenticity of your dream and your commitment to achieving it, they are more likely to join your journey and remain loyal through its ups and downs.

Building Resilience: The Entrepreneur's Armor

The path of entrepreneurship is strewn with both triumphs and trials. Resilience is not just a useful trait; it's essential armor for anyone daring to forge their own path in business. This resilience comes from an unshakeable belief in your mission and a clear understanding that setbacks are not endpoints but learning points.

Cultivate resilience by setting realistic expectations and preparing for the inevitable ebbs and flows of business life. Celebrate your victories, no matter how small, and learn from your defeats without letting them define you. Maintain a network of support—mentors, peers, friends—who can offer advice, share their experiences, and remind you that you're not alone in this journey.

Continuous Learning: The Lifelong Student

The world changes at a dizzying pace. New technologies, shifting market trends, and evolving consumer preferences—all demand a commitment to continuous learning. The most successful entrepreneurs are those who remain students for life. They read widely, listen eagerly, and are always tuned into learning opportunities.

Invest time and resources in upgrading your skills and deepening your knowledge. Attend workshops, take courses, read books, and stay connected with industry leaders. Each piece of knowledge adds a layer of strength to your business strategy, allowing you to adapt and thrive in an ever-changing landscape.

Taking Action: The Final Push

Now, as we part ways in this book, the real work begins. It's time to move from planning to action, from dreaming to doing. Start small if you must, but start. Take that first step, then another, then another.

Momentum will build with each move forward, and before you know it, you'll be running.

Launching your business is just the beginning. Each day will bring new challenges, new opportunities to make a difference, and new chances to redefine success. Keep your goals clear, your commitment unwavering, and your actions aligned with your values. Be bold in your pursuits, ethical in your practices, and kind in your interactions.

Your Entrepreneurial Legacy: More than Just Business

Finally, remember that entrepreneurship is more than just a commercial venture; it's a legacy you build every day. It's about the impact you have on your customers, your community, and perhaps, the world. What will your legacy be? How will your business change lives? Keep these questions at the heart of your entrepreneurial journey.

This is your moment. You have everything you need to take action, now, it's time to start. Remember, progress is built one step at a time. Keep learning, stay connected to your vision, and celebrate every small victory along the way.

Your journey begins now!

Interested in more books by Mitche?

https://amzn.to/4f4ziAL

Interested in hiring Mitche to speak?

https://powermarketing101.com/speaking

Interested in joining Mitche's MasterMind?

https://powermarketing101.com/coaching